Poet and Peasant
and Other Great Overtures
in Full Score

Franz von Suppé

DOVER PUBLICATIONS, INC.
Mineola, New York

Bibliographical Note

This Dover edition, first published in 2001, is a new compilation of five works originally published separately, all n.d. C.F.W. Siegel, Leipzig, originally published the Overture to *Morning, Noon and Night in Vienna*. August Cranz, Leipzig, originally published the overtures to *The Beautiful Galatea* and *Light Cavalry*, and the independent *Vienna Jubilee Overture*. Josef Aibl, Munich, originally published the overture to *Poet and Peasant*.

The publisher's note, p. iii, is drawn in part from Peter Branscombe's Suppé entry in Volume 18 of *The New Grove Dictionary of Music and Musicians*, edited by Stanley Sadie (© Macmillan Publishers Limited 1980).

We are grateful to the Walter W. Gerboth Music Library, Brooklyn College, NY, for the loan of these rare scores for republication.

International Standard Book Number: 0-486-41397-7

Manufactured in the United States of America
Dover Publications, Inc., 31 East 2nd Street, Mineola, N.Y. 11501

NOTE

Born Francesco Ezechiele Ermenegildo Cavaliere Suppé Demelli, Franz von Suppé (1819–1895) is the earliest Viennese composer of musical farces whose works still survive as either viable stage works or popular overtures. His mastery of the classical operetta, following the lead of Jacques Offenbach, greatly influenced the development of Austrian and German light music up to the middle of the 20th century. Suppé's light, fluent, elegant style and superb orchestrations characterize the best of his work.

Until 1845 Suppé wrote well over twenty scores for the Theater in der Josefstadt, Vienna, then moved to the Theater an der Wien where he served as Kapellmeister for the next seventeen years, conducting many important operatic performances including, notably, Meyerbeer works with Jenny Lind. Turning out a series of theater scores of varying success—including overtures, incidental music, opera parodies and the like—Suppé moved to Vienna's Kaitheater in 1862, then to the Carltheater in 1865. His career there as Kapellmeister ended with retirement in 1882, although he continued to compose, devoting a part of his attention to large-scale sacred works, including a requiem and three masses.

CONTENTS

INSTRUMENTATION

of the five works in this volume

Piccolo
Flute
2 Oboes
2 Clarinets
2 Bassoons

4 Horns
3 Trumpets
3 Trombones

Ophicleide
(in *Poet and Peasant* only)

Timpani
Percussion

Harp
(in *Poet and Peasant* only)

Violins I, II
Violas
Cellos
Basses

A piano reduction of the full score is provided at the bottom of each page of the three overtures originally published by August Cranz: *Light Cavalry, The Beautiful Galatea,* and *Vienna Jubilee Overture.*

Poet and Peasant
and Other Great Overtures

Overture to
Morning, Noon and Night in Vienna
Ein Morgen, ein Mittag und ein Abend in Wien (1844)

Andante amoroso.(M.M. ♪ = 92.)

Andante amoroso.(M.M. ♪ = 92.)

Morning, Noon & Night / 3

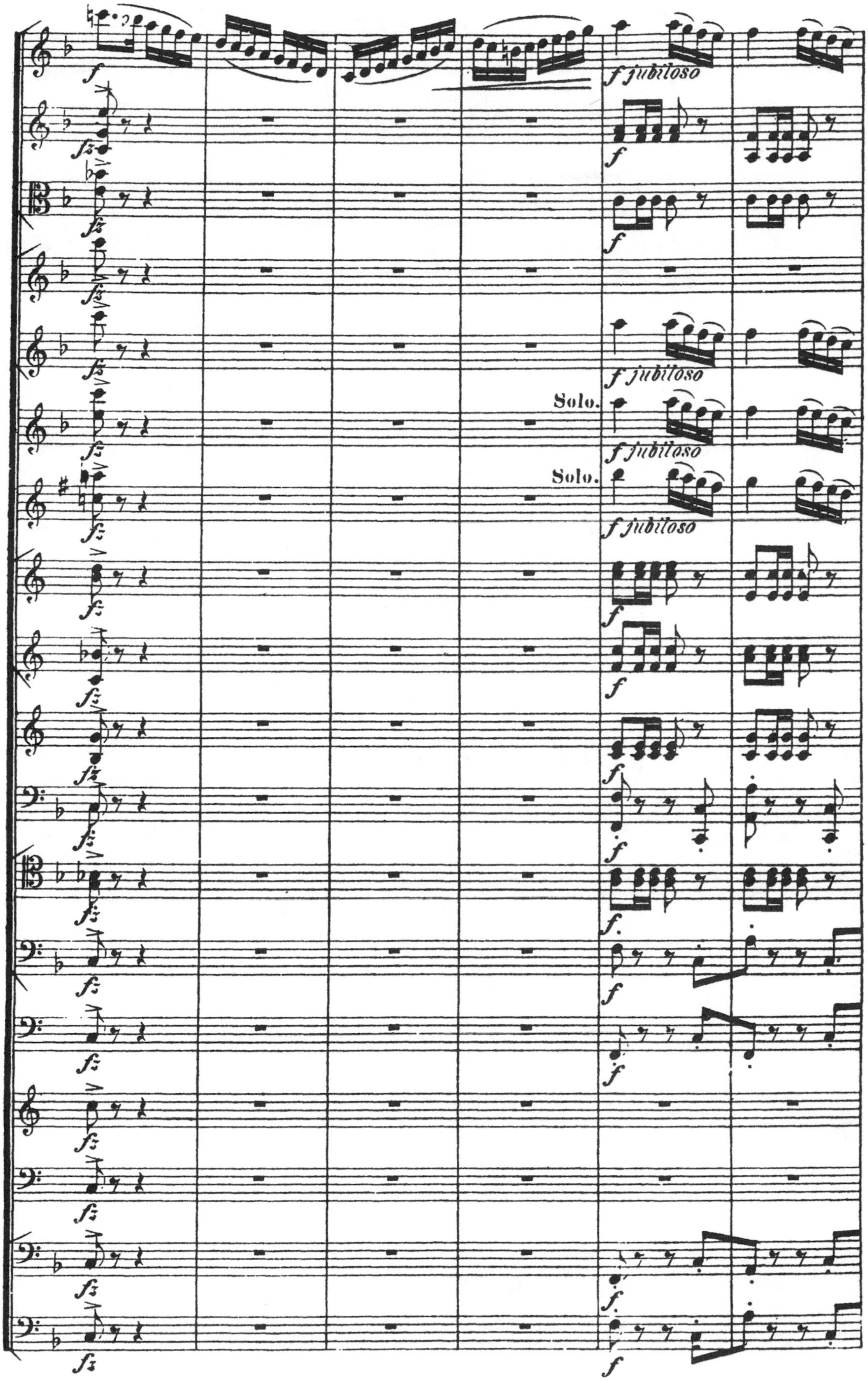
f jubiloso
f jubiloso
Solo.
f jubiloso
Solo.
f jubiloso

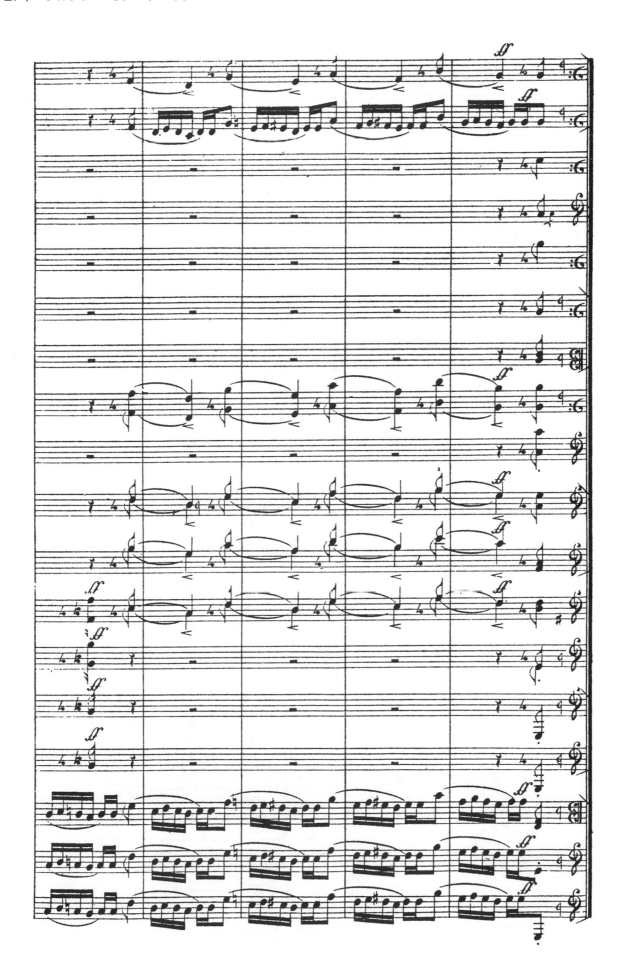

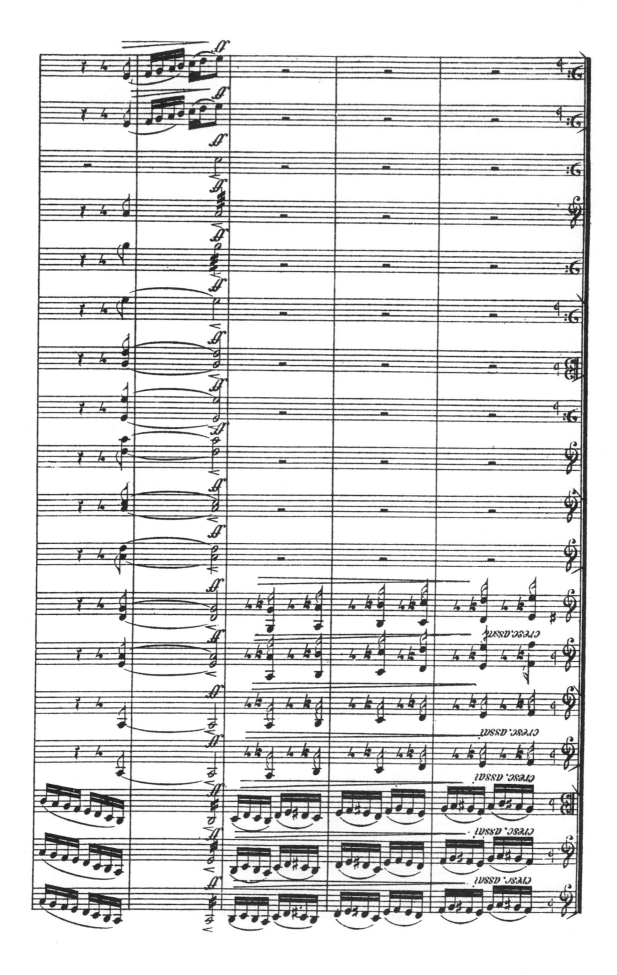

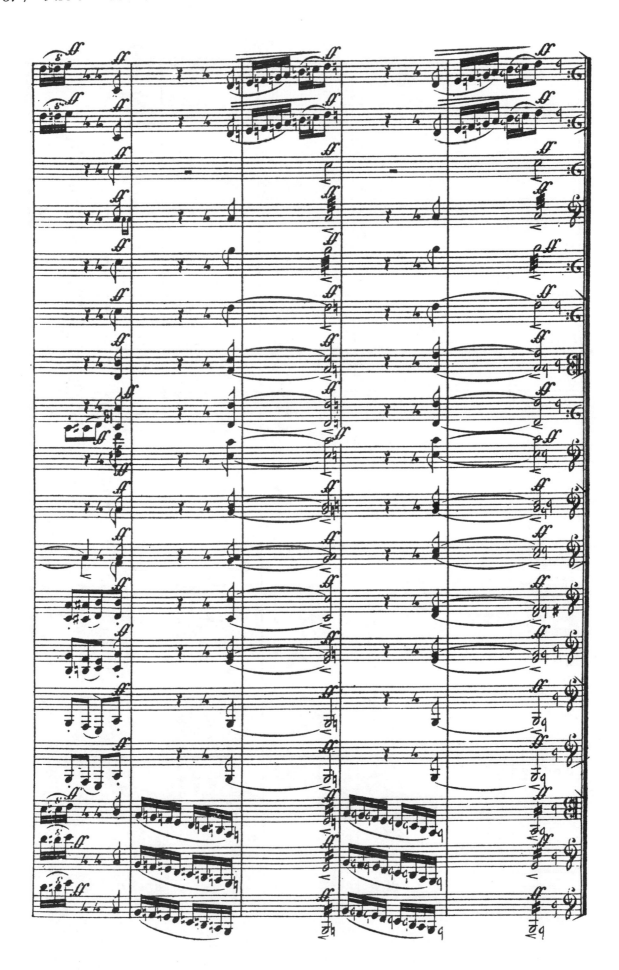

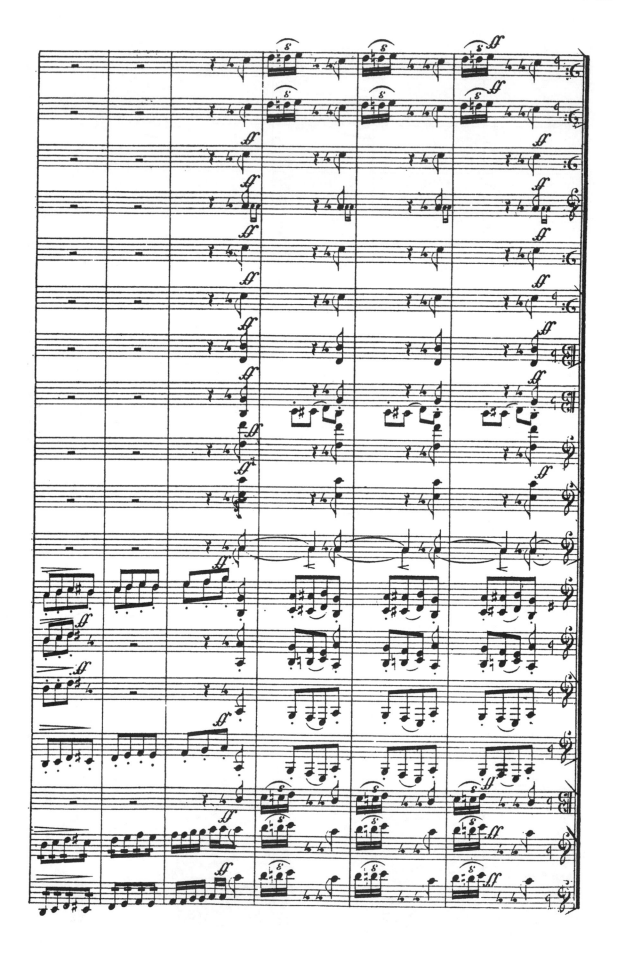

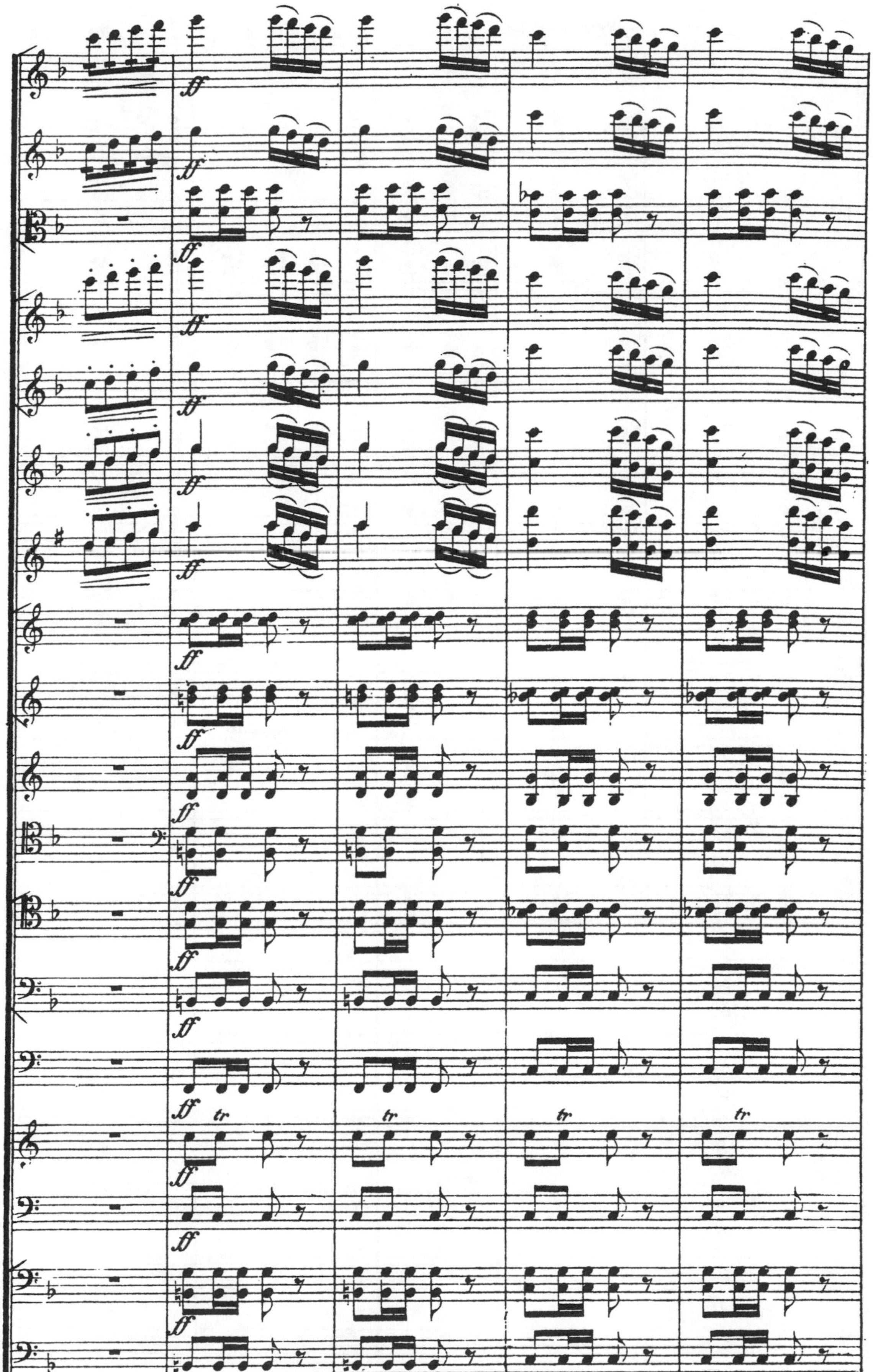
ff
tr

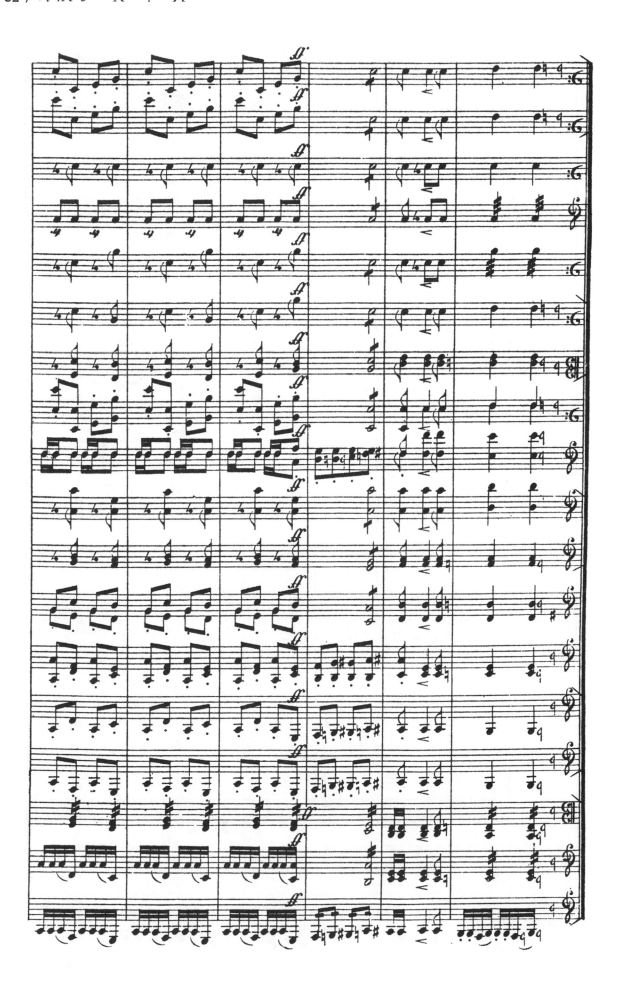

Overture to

Poet and Peasant

Dichter und Bauer (1846)

Allegro.

Allegretto.

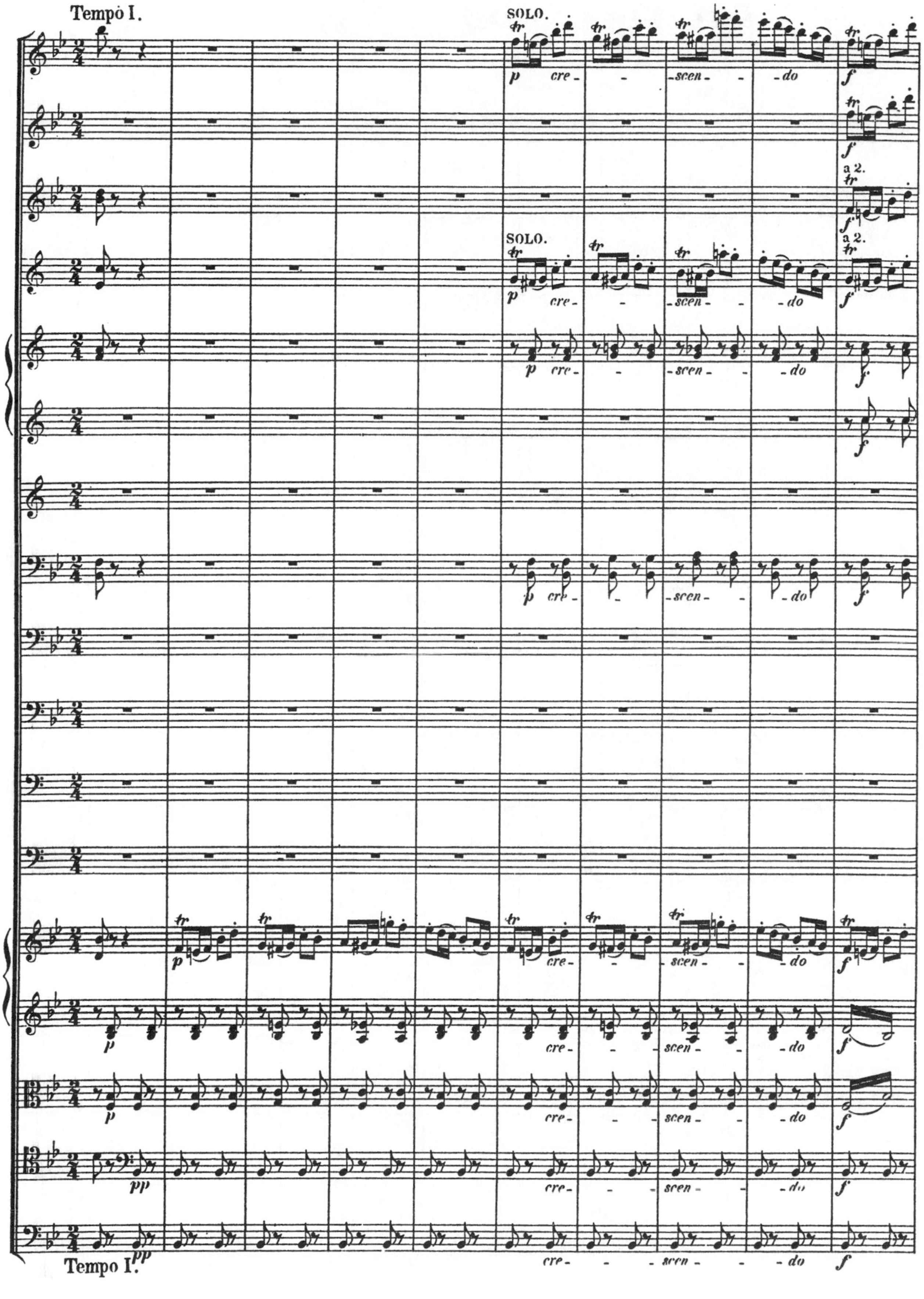
Tempo I.
SOLO.
tr
p cre - - scen - - do
f
a 2.
SOLO.
Tempo I.
pp

Overture to
The Beautiful Galatea
Die schöne Galatea (1865).

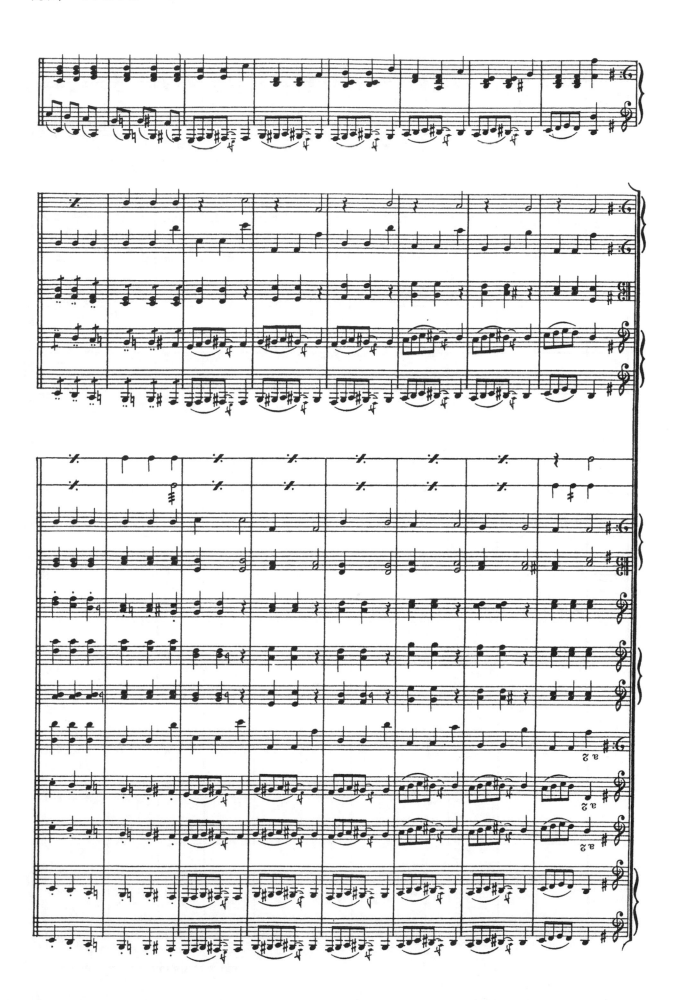

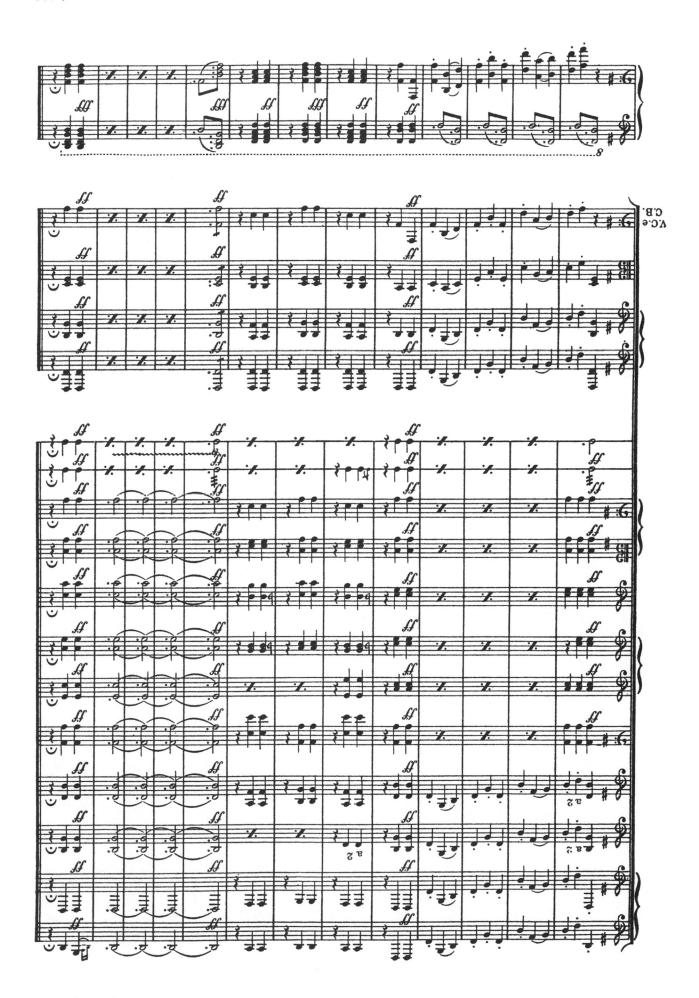

Overture to

Light Cavalry

Die leichte Kavallerie (1866)

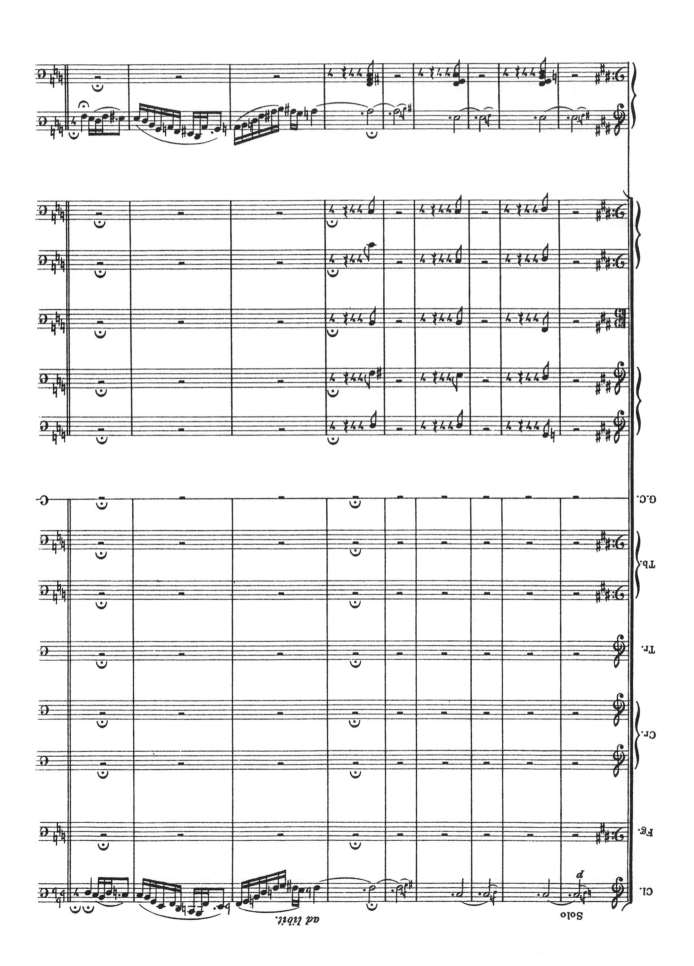

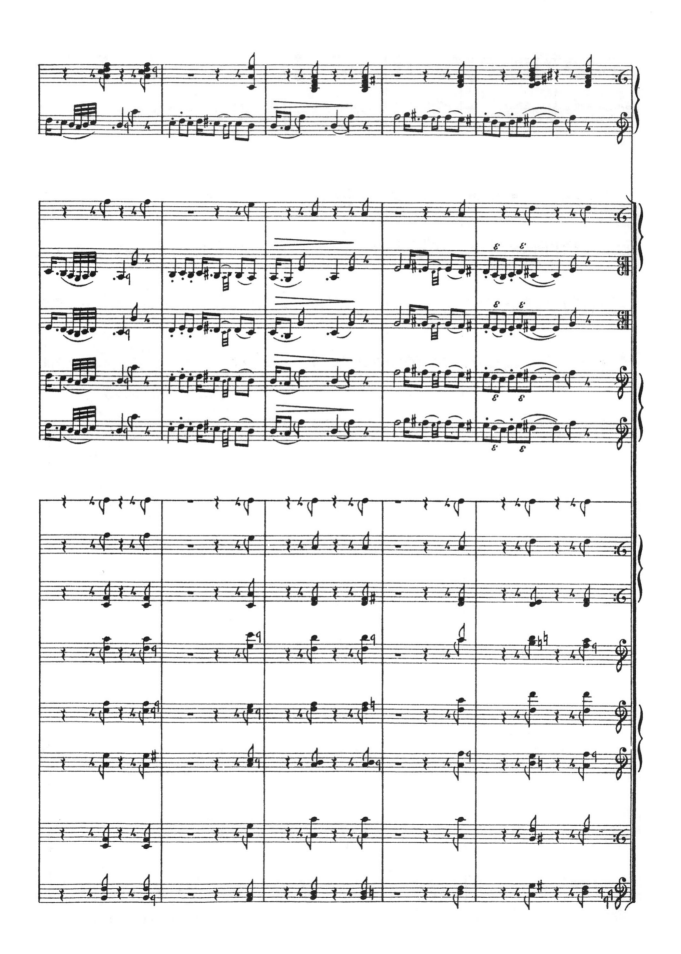

Tempo I (Allegretto brillante)
p
Tempo I (Allegretto brillante)
Tempo I (Allegretto brillante)
p

Vienna Jubilee Overture

Wiener Jubel-Ouverture

Vienna Jubilee / 173

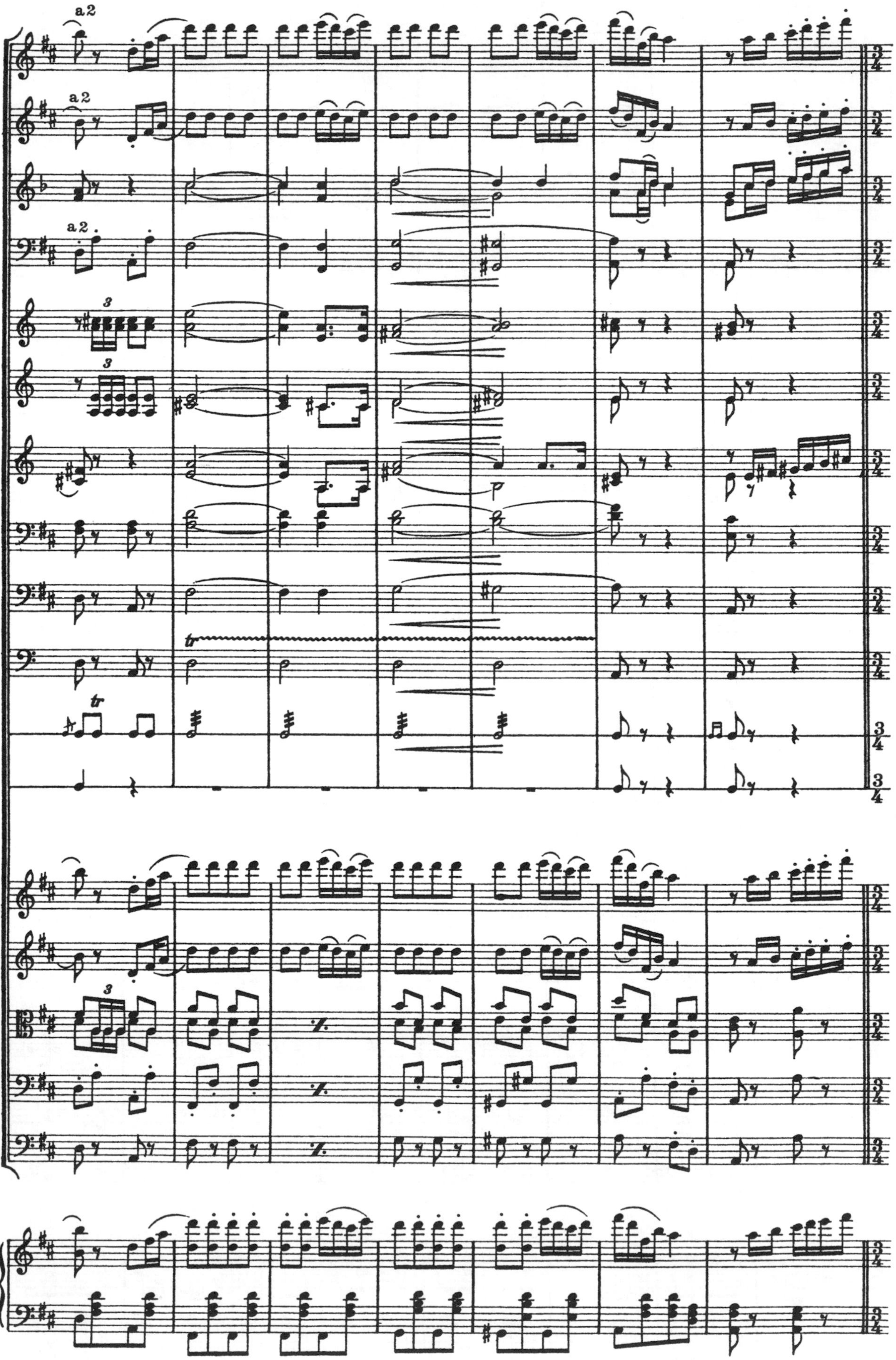
a 2
a 2
a 2
tr
tr
3
3
3

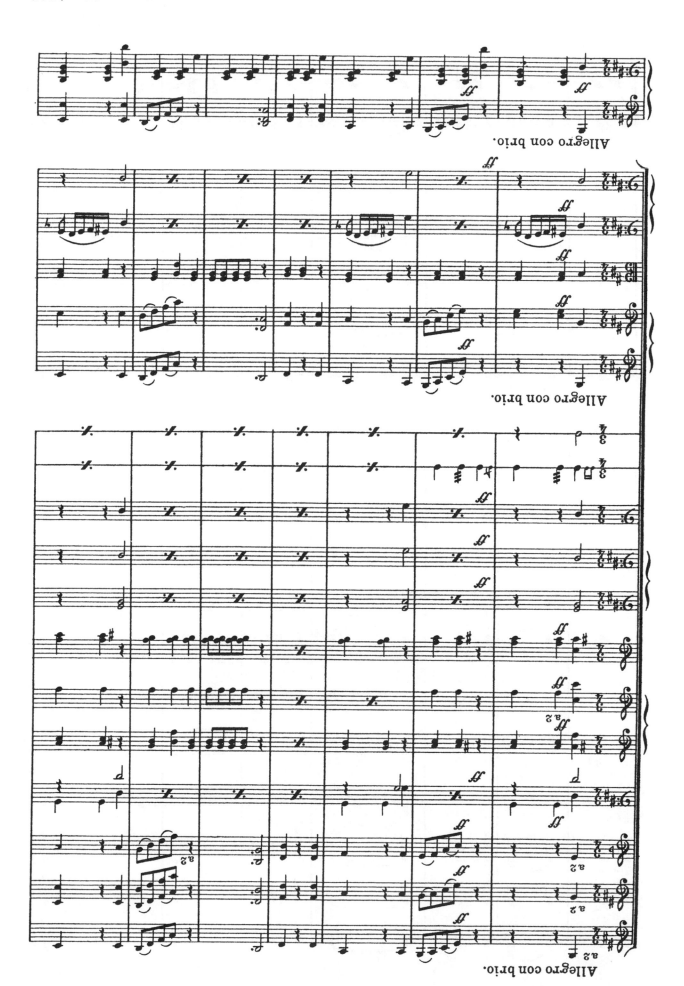

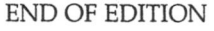

END OF EDITION